Sports Illustrated KIDS

HOCKEY'S RECORD BREAKERS

BY SHANE FREDERICK

CAPSTONE PRESS
a capstone imprint

Sports Illustrated Kids Record Breakers is published in 2017
by Capstone Press, 1710 Roe Crest Drive, North Mankato, Minnesota 56003
www.mycapstone.com

Sports Illustrated Kids is a trademark of Time Inc. Used with permission.

Library of Congress Cataloging-in-Publication Data is available on the Library of Congress website.
ISBN 978-1-5157-3758-2 (library binding)
ISBN 978-1-5157-3762-9 (paperback)
ISBN 978-1-5157-3771-1 (eBook PDF)

Editorial Credits
Nick Healy, editor; Veronica Scott, designer; Eric Gohl, media researcher;
Gene Bentdahl, production specialist

AP Photo: Paul Warner, 23, Tom Pidgeon, 22; Getty Images: Bruce Bennett, 7, 9 (top), 11 (top), 26, 27, Ron Bull, 8, Stringer/Jeff Zelevansky, 10; Newscom: Icon SMI/IHA, 12–13 (bottom), 14, Reuters/Joe Giza, 20; Shutterstock: Adam Vilimek, cover; Sports Illustrated: Damian Strohmeyer, 13 (top left), David E. Klutho, 6, 11 (bottom), 15, 17, 19, 28, 29, Heinz Kluetmeier, 21, 24, Hy Peskin, 9 (bottom), John G. Zimmerman, 18, Manny Millan, 25, Simon Bruty, 16, Tony Triolo, 4, 13 (right)

Design Elements: Shutterstock

Printed in the United States of America.
010054S17

TABLE OF CONTENTS

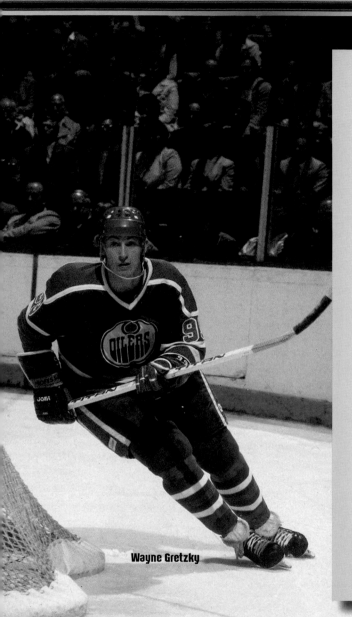

Wayne Gretzky

Wayne Gretzky set many records during his years as an Edmonton Oilers superstar. He racked up the most points in a season (215 in 1985–86). He netted the most goals in a season (92 in 1981–82). And he dished out the most assists in a game (seven, three times). He was indeed "The Great One."

On October 15, 1989, Gretzky was in Edmonton but as a member of the Los Angeles Kings, to whom he'd been traded in 1988. That night he was on the verge of breaking pro hockey's ultimate individual record and becoming the all-time leading point scorer.

GRETZKY FINISHED HIS CAREER WITH 2,857 POINTS. HIS ASSIST TOTAL OF 1,963 ALONE COULD STAND AS THE ALL-TIME SCORING RECORD.

Gretzky trailed Gordie Howe's record of 1,850 points by just one when the game began. Early on, he assisted on a goal scored by Bernie Nicholls to tie the mark. The Oilers held Gretzky in check for much of the rest of the game and held a late 4-3 lead. As time ran short, the Kings pulled their goalie for an extra attacker. Gretzky quickly broke the record with a game-tying goal, coming with just a minute left to play. The Edmonton crowd exploded in cheers for the former Oiler. After a long celebration, the game went into overtime, during which—you guessed it—Gretzky scored the game-winning goal.

RECORD BREAKERS

ON ANY GIVEN NIGHT IN THE NATIONAL HOCKEY LEAGUE (NHL), A PLAYER OR A TEAM HAS A CHANCE TO CHASE OR EVEN BREAK A RECORD. SOME RECORDS FALL REGULARLY. OTHERS STAND FOR GENERATIONS BEFORE THEY ARE TOUCHED. AND OTHERS—LIKE GRETZKY'S— SEEM LIKE THEY'LL NEVER BE BROKEN.

CAREER POINTS

1. **Wayne Gretzky** (Oilers, Kings, Blues, Rangers)	**2,857**
2. **Mark Messier** (Oilers, Rangers, Canucks)	**1,887**
3. **Jaromir Jagr** (Penguins, Capitals, Rangers, Flyers, Stars, Bruins, Devils, Panthers)	**1,868**
4. **Gordie Howe** (Red Wings, Whalers)	**1,850**
5. **Ron Francis** (Whalers, Penguins, Hurricanes, Maple Leafs)	**1,798**

Jagr stats through 2015-16 season

On his way to winning the Hart Trophy as the NHL's most valuable player (MVP) in 2015–16, Chicago Blackhawks winger Patrick Kane strung together an impressive streak. He scored at least one point in 26 consecutive games.

Keeping the streak alive required that he get at least one goal or assist in each game. In some games Kane scored three or four points. Other nights he kept it going only with an assist on an empty-net goal. Kane's scoring streak was the longest ever by an American-born player and the longest by any player in 23 years.

Patrick Kane

As impressive as Kane's streak was, it did not come close to matching the longest streak in NHL history. That record belongs to Wayne Gretzky, who scored in 51 straight games during the 1983–84 season. Gretzky had a goal and an assist on opening night October 5, 1983, and wasn't blanked until January 28, 1984. Along the way, he scored 61 goals and assisted on 92 others for 153 points. He finished the season with 205 points.

Kane, who had 40 points during his run, ranks 11th on the NHL's list of longest scoring streaks.

SUPER SCORER

When it comes to scoring, few players have come close to Wayne Gretzky. The Great One is the only player in NHL history to record 200 or more points in a season, and he did it four times. That includes a 215-point season in 1985–86. Mario Lemieux of the Pittsburgh Penguins scored 199 points in 1988–89.

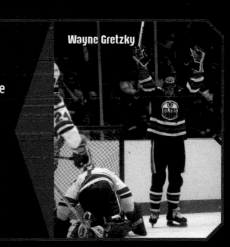

Wayne Gretzky

LONGEST POINT STREAKS

1. **Wayne Gretzky** (Oilers), 1983–84	**51 games**
2. **Mario Lemieux** (Penguins), 1989–90	**46 games**
3. **Wayne Gretzky** (Oilers), 1985–86	**39 games**
4. **Mats Sundin** (Nordiques), 1992–93	**30 games**
4. **Wayne Gretzky** (Oilers), 1982–83	**30 games**

PERFECT 10

Two periods were in the books, and Darryl Sittler of the Toronto Maple Leafs already had three goals and four assists. It was February 7, 1976, and Sittler knew he needed just one point to tie an old record for points in a single game. Forty-four seconds into the third period, Sittler scored a fourth goal, becoming the third NHL player to put up eight points in a game.

Darryl Sittler

The great Maurice "Rocket" Richard of the Montreal Canadiens had scored eight points during a game in 1944. Ten years later the Canadiens' Bert Olmstead had done the same. When Sittler matched them, more than 19 minutes remained in the Leafs' game against the Boston Bruins. Sittler broke the record midway through the period, ripping the puck past goalie Dave Reece. Then, with three and a half minutes to go, Sittler scored again for a 10th point!

Sittler's record has stood for more than 40 years. During that time NHL players have notched eight-point games 11 more times. The Edmonton Oilers' Sam Gagner had the last one in 2012.

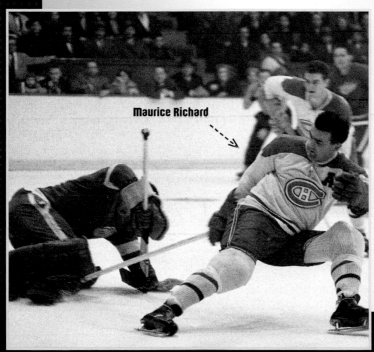

Maurice Richard

NO AVERAGE JOE

Joe Malone set the record for most goals in a single game way back in 1920. Playing for the Quebec Bulldogs, Malone scored seven goals. There have been seven six-goal games in NHL history, most recently Sittler during his 10-point game. The Detroit Red Wings' Johan Franzen became the latest to join the five-goal club in 2011.

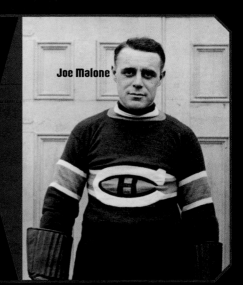

Joe Malone

WINNER, WINNER

It was a record so nice that Jaromir Jagr broke it twice. In October 2013, while playing for the New Jersey Devils, Jagr got loose on a breakaway. He fired the puck past Tampa Bay Lightning goaltender Ben Bishop for the Devils' second goal of the game. New Jersey ended up winning 2-1, so Jagr's score was the game-winning goal. It was the 119th game-winner of Jagr's long career, one more than Hall-of-Famer Phil Esposito and the NHL record.

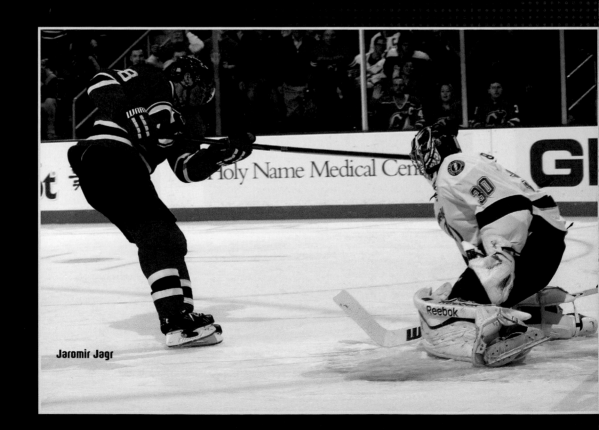

Jaromir Jagr

Phil Esposito

Or so he thought.

Shortly after the game, statisticians combed through the books and discovered that another all-time great, Gordie Howe, actually owned the record with 121 game-winners. Jagr would have to keep going to reach the real record.

About two months later, Jagr did it again. His second-period goal in a 5-2 victory over the Ottawa Senators stood up as the game-winner. It was his fourth such goal of the season and the 122nd game-winner of his career. Through the 2015–16 season, the aged star had 133 game-winning goals.

CLUTCH GOALS

A game-winning goal is the goal that gives a team one more goal than its opponent. It can come at any time in the game. For instance, in a 5-2 game, the victorious team's third goal is the winner. The most dramatic winners, however, come in overtime. Jagr holds the record with 19 regular-season overtime winners. The Chicago Blackhawks' Jonathan Toews and the Tampa Bay Lightning's Steven Stamkos share the single-season record of five.

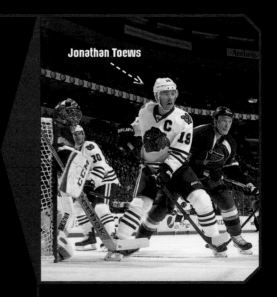

Jonathan Toews

Bobby Orr burst onto the ice in 1966 as an 18-year-old for the Boston Bruins. In just three seasons, he was revolutionizing the position of defenseman, doing things no blueliner had ever done before. Where once defenders stuck with the job of defending, Orr added offense. He carried the puck deep into the attacking zone, looking to make plays. He scored goals—lots of them—and set up his teammates for even more.

During the 1968–69 season, Orr scored 21 goals and finished the season with 64 points. He surpassed Chicago Blackhawk Pierre Pilote's record of 57 points by a defenseman, set just four years earlier. As impressive as that performance was, however, Orr shocked the hockey world a year later. That season he nearly doubled his total, scoring 33 goals and compiling 120 points. Orr led the NHL in point-scoring that season, something he would do one other time (135 points in 1974–75). No other defenseman had done that before, and none has since. Orr's defenseman record of 139 points in 1970–71 may never be matched.

Bobby Orr

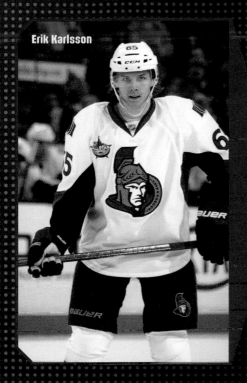

Erik Karlsson

AFTER ORR

AFTER ORR

Bobby Orr's offensive genius inspired many more defensemen to get in on the scoring. In 2015–16, the Ottawa Senators' Erik Karlsson scored 82 points, which ranked fourth in the NHL. It was the first time since Paul Coffey's 138-point season 30 years earlier that a defenseman ranked among the league's top five in points.

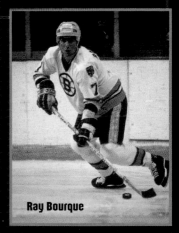

Ray Bourque

CAREER POINTS BY A DEFENSEMAN

1. Ray Bourque (Bruins, Avalanche)	**1,579**
2. Paul Coffey (Oilers, Penguins, Kings, Red Wings, Whalers, Flyers, Blackhawks, Hurricanes, Bruins)	**1,531**
3. Al MacInnis (Flames, Blues)	**1,274**
4. Phil Housley (Sabres, Jets, Blues, Flames, Devils, Capitals, Blackhawks, Maple Leafs)	**1,232**
5. Larry Murphy (Kings, Capitals, North Stars, Penguins, Maple Leafs, Red Wings)	**1,216**

MEAN STREAK

Glenn Hall had a strong stomach and a stronger face. Each night, before getting between the pipes to play goaltender, he got so excited that he would throw up. Then he would chug a glass of orange juice and hit the ice. Playing in an era when goalies didn't wear protective masks, Hall received 250 stitches to close cuts on his face. Still, he rarely got a break from the action.

Glenn Hall

For a stretch of seven years, Hall never left the net. He played in 502 consecutive games (551 counting playoff games), setting a record that likely will never be broken.

Hall kept his record run alive even as he changed teams, going from the Detroit Red Wings to the Chicago Blackhawks in 1957. Strangely, Hall's streak ended not with another puck to the face but because of a back injury suffered while adjusting his equipment. The streak ended in 1962, but his career wasn't close to finished. He played his last NHL game with the St. Louis Blues in 1971. In all, he appeared in more than 900 games over 18 seasons.

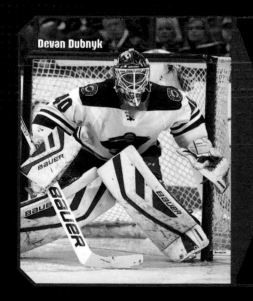

Devan Dubnyk

SHORT STREAKS

In 2014–15 the Minnesota Wild wanted goaltending help and traded for Devan Dubnyk. He was just what the team needed. Dubnyk started 39 games in a row before getting a night off. It was the longest streak since **Evgeni Nabokov** started 43 straight for the San Jose Sharks in 2007–08. Hardly Glenn **Hall** territory.

THE LONGEST PLAYING STREAK FOR A NON-GOALIE IS 964 GAMES BY DOUG JARVIS. THE CENTER SPREAD HIS STREAK OVER STINTS WITH THREE TEAMS: THE MONTREAL CANADIENS, WASHINGTON CAPITALS, AND HARTFORD WHALERS.

WINNING TIME

Washington Capitals goaltender Braden Holtby had 47 victories to his name late in the 2015–16 season when his team went to St. Louis to play the Blues. He knew that somewhere high up in the arena watching him that night was Blues assistant general manager Martin Brodeur. With another win Holtby would tie Brodeur for most goaltending victories in a single season.

Holtby wasn't fazed. He stopped 19 of 20 shots as the Capitals defeated the Blues. With his 48th win, he tied Brodeur's impressive feat from 2006–07. The two goalies still share the record.

Brodeur had done something similar, breaking the record of Bernie Parent with Parent in the building to watch. Parent won 47 games for the Philadelphia Flyers during the 1973–74 season.

Braden Holtby

Parent had 13 losses and 12 ties during his record season. Holtby and Brodeur achieved their record totals in an era with no ties. The NHL did not start playing overtime periods until 1983. Four-on-four and three-on-three overtime rules, as well as shootouts, gave them extra chances to win (and lose). Holtby had nine regulation losses and seven overtime/shootout losses along with his 48 wins. Brodeur had 23 losses and seven overtime/shootout losses.

HIGH BAR

There's never been a busier goalie than Sam LoPresti was on a night in Boston in 1941. Playing for the Chicago Blackhawks, LoPresti made an NHL-record 80 saves, facing a whopping 83 shots. He couldn't pull off the victory, however, as the Bruins scored a late goal to win 3-2.

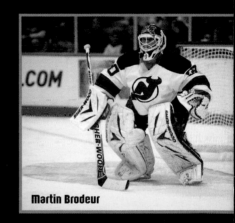

Martin Brodeur

CAREER WINS BY A GOALTENDER

1. Martin Brodeur (Devils, Blues)	691
2. Patrick Roy (Canadiens, Avalanche)	551
3. Ed Belfour (Blackhawks, Stars, Maple Leafs, Panthers, Sharks)	484
4. Curtis Joseph (Blues, Maple Leafs, Oilers, Red Wings, Coyotes, Flames)	454
5. Terry Sawchuk (Red Wings, Maple Leafs, Bruins, Kings, Rangers)	447

NO GOALS ALLOWED

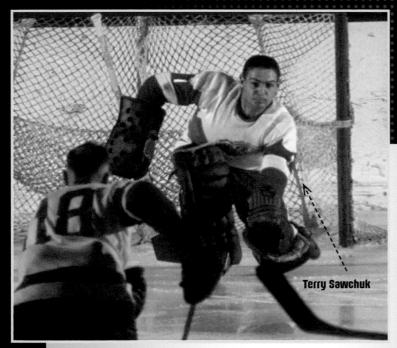

Terry Sawchuk

For decades, goaltender Terry Sawchuk's record of 103 shutouts looked to be unbreakable. But then along came Martin Brodeur.

Brodeur owned the New Jersey Devils' net for 20 years, rarely taking time off to rest. He racked up many records, including games played in goal and most wins. In December 2009—40 years after Sawchuk set his mark—Brodeur broke the record. He blanked Sidney Crosby and the Pittsburgh Penguins for his 104th shutout.

The 37-year-old Brodeur stopped 35 shots that night, but he also got help from his teammates. They put their own bodies in front of screaming pucks, blocking shots to keep the shutout alive. He also got a little luck when a Crosby shot went off the post with about 90 seconds remaining in the game.

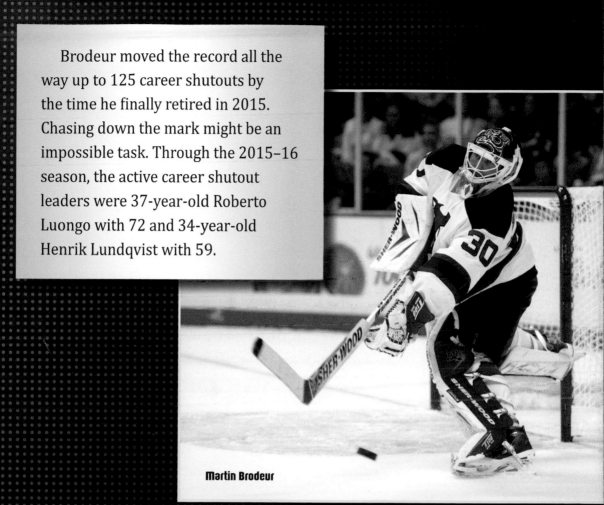

Brodeur moved the record all the way up to 125 career shutouts by the time he finally retired in 2015. Chasing down the mark might be an impossible task. Through the 2015–16 season, the active career shutout leaders were 37-year-old Roberto Luongo with 72 and 34-year-old Henrik Lundqvist with 59.

Martin Brodeur

CAREER SHUTOUTS

1. Martin Brodeur (Devils, Blues)	125
2. Terry Sawchuk (Red Wings, Maple Leafs, Bruins, Kings, Rangers)	103
3. George Hainsworth (Canadiens, Maple Leafs)	94
4. Glenn Hall (Blackhawks, Red Wings, Blues)	84
5. Jacques Plante (Canadiens, Rangers, Blues, Maple Leafs, Bruins)	82

KEEP OUT!

It was New Year's Eve in 2003, and Brian Boucher got a rare chance to start in goal for the Phoenix Coyotes. The backup made the most of his opportunity. He shut out the Los Angeles Kings that night, 4-0.

Boucher was back in goal for the next game and got another shutout. Then another. And another. And another. After five shutouts in a row, Boucher had a modern-day NHL record.

Sometimes it takes a little dose of good luck to get a shutout. For Boucher, a little bad luck ended the streak. As he was going for his sixth straight shutout, the Atlanta Thrashers ended the run on a fluke. They scored when a passed puck bounced off the chest of one of Boucher's teammates and into the net.

Brian Boucher

But for the previous 332 minutes, 1 second of playing time, nothing had gotten past Boucher. The streak outlasted the previous record of 309 minutes, 21 seconds without giving up a goal. That mark was set in 1949 by the Montreal Canadiens' Bill Durnan.

OLD-TIME HOCKEY

The NHL's modern era began in 1943 with new rules to speed up the game and increase scoring. Before that, goals were harder to come by, resulting in more shutouts. Brian Boucher's record fell short of two "dead-puck era" records. Alec Connell of the 1927–28 Ottawa Senators holds the all-time record of 461 minutes, 29 seconds. His streak included six shutouts.

Patrick Roy

CAREER PLAYOFF SHUTOUTS

1. Martin Brodeur (Devils, Blues)	**24**
2. Patrick Roy (Canadiens, Avalanche)	**23**
3. Curtis Joseph (Blues, Oilers, Maple Leafs, Red Wings, Flames, Coyotes)	**16**
4. Chris Osgood (Red Wings, Islanders, Blues)	**15**
5. Jacques Plante (Canadiens, Rangers, Blues, Maple Leafs, Bruins)	**14**
5. Dominik Hasek (Blackhawks, Sabres, Red Wings, Senators)	**14**
5. Ed Belfour (Blackhawks, Sharks, Stars, Maple Leafs, Panthers)	**14**

With two games left in the 1995–96 season, the Detroit Red Wings had already tied the NHL record for most wins in a season with 60. Determined to set a new mark, they crushed the visiting Chicago Blackhawks 5-3. The Red Wings out-shot the Blackhawks 45-14 that night for win number 61. Paul Coffey scored two goals and assisted on another, and longtime captain Steve Yzerman assisted on three goals.

Two nights later, Detroit dominated the Dallas Stars 5-1 for its 62nd victory. The Red Wings finished the regular season with a 62–13–7 record. They surpassed the 1976–77 Montreal Canadiens, one the NHL's greatest teams, by two wins. Unlike that Canadiens team, the Red Wings did not win the Stanley Cup championship after their record-setting regular season.

Dino Ciccarelli of the record-setting Red Wings

For Red Wings coach Scotty Bowman, breaking the single-season wins record must have seemed like déjà vu. That's because Bowman had also coached the 1976–77 Canadiens two decades earlier.

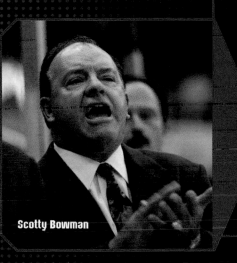

Scotty Bowman

SCOTTY AND STANLEY

Scotty Bowman holds the records for most coaching wins (1,244) and most Stanley Cup championships by a coach. His teams won nine Cups, including five with the Canadiens (four in a row from 1976 to 1979), one with the Penguins, and three with the Red Wings. The Canadiens hold the record for most championships in franchise history with 24.

MOST TEAM WINS IN A SEASON

1. Detroit Red Wings, 1995–96	62
2. Montreal Canadiens, 1976–77	60
3. Montreal Canadiens, 1977–78	59
4. Detroit Red Wings, 2005–06	58
4. Montreal Canadiens, 1975–76	58

IN THEIR FIRST SEASON AS A FRANCHISE, THE WASHINGTON CAPITALS WENT 8-67-5, THE WORST RECORD EVER BY AN NHL TEAM.

AWESOME OFFENSE

It was a night no goaltender could enjoy. On December 11, 1985, the high-flying Edmonton Oilers traveled to Chicago to face the Blackhawks. The two teams put on a goal-scoring display no one had seen in several decades.

The Oilers won the game 12-9, and the combined 21 goals tied the NHL record for the most goals in a single game. The last time it had happened was in 1920, when the Montreal Canadiens defeated the Toronto St. Patricks 14-7.

Surprisingly, Oilers superstar Wayne Gretzky did not score a goal in the game. But he assisted on seven of them! Two of his teammates, Glenn Anderson and Jari Kurri, notched hat tricks. Anderson also had three assists for a six-point night. The Blackhawks' Troy Murray notched two goals and two assists.

Jari Kurri

In the Canadiens' drubbing of the St. Patricks 65 years earlier, Newsy Lalonde scored six goals for the winners.

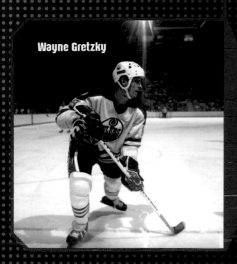

Wayne Gretzky

GREATEST SHOW ON ICE

The Edmonton Oilers of the early 1980s scored goals like no other team. From 1981 to 1986, Edmonton produced the top five scoring seasons in NHL history—and the only five 400-goal seasons. Tops was the 1983–84 team's total of 446 goals, an average of 5.58 per game.

THE MOST GOALS SCORED BY ONE TEAM IN A SINGLE GAME WAS 16 BY THE MONTREAL CANADIENS, WHO DEFEATED THE QUEBEC BULLDOGS 16-3 IN 1920.

THE NHL'S LONGEST GAMES

1. Red Wings 1, Maroons 0; March 24, 1936; 2:56:30 (6 OTs)

2. Maple Leafs 1, Bruins 0; April 3, 1933; 2:44:46 (6 OTs)

3. Flyers 2, Penguins 1; May 4, 2000; 2:32:01 (5 OTs)

4. Ducks 4, Stars 3; April 24, 2003; 2:20:48 (5 OTs)

5. Penguins 3, Capitals 2; April 24, 1996; 2:19:15 (4 OTs)

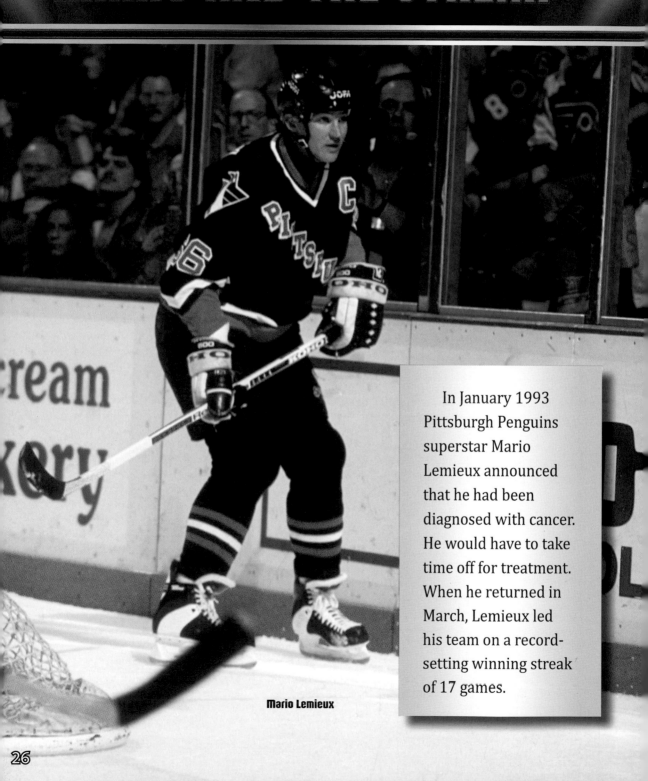

MARIO AND THE STREAK

In January 1993 Pittsburgh Penguins superstar Mario Lemieux announced that he had been diagnosed with cancer. He would have to take time off for treatment. When he returned in March, Lemieux led his team on a record-setting winning streak of 17 games.

Mario Lemieux

The streak started with Lemieux's first game back in his home rink, a 3-2 win over the Boston Bruins. Along the way, Pittsburgh won two overtime games, getting game-winners from Jaromir Jagr and Ulf Samuelsson. But it was Lemieux who carried the team on his back for the majority of the wins.

Super Mario scored an amazing 60 points during the streak, including 27 goals. There was a four-goal, two-assist performance in the fourth win and a four-goal, one-assist effort the next night. In the 16th win, which broke the old record, Lemieux scored five times.

The streak ended on the final day of the regular season. It ended with a 6-6 tie with the New Jersey Devils.

LOSING IS NOT AN OPTION

For nearly three months during the 1979–80 season, the Philadelphia Flyers couldn't lose. After starting the season with one win and one loss, they played their next 35 games without losing again. They won 25 times and tied 10 times over that stretch. That surpassed the previous unbeaten streak record of 28 games set by the 1977–78 Canadiens.

THE LONGEST WINLESS STREAK IN NHL HISTORY WAS 30 GAMES, A STRETCH OF 0–23–7 BY THE 1980–81 WINNIPEG JETS. TWO TEAMS SHARE THE RECORD FOR THE LONGEST LOSING STREAK. THE 1974–75 WASHINGTON CAPITALS AND THE 1992–93 SAN JOSE SHARKS LOST 17 GAMES IN A ROW.

THE FUTURE

Some of Wayne Gretzky's record numbers may never be surpassed. That doesn't mean players aren't willing to give chase.

At the end of the 2015–16 season, Alexander Ovechkin of the Washington Capitals and Sidney Crosby of the Pittsburgh Penguins were both closing in on 1,000 career points. Eleven seasons into their NHL careers, each player ranked among the top 100 all-time point scorers.

In 2007 Crosby became the youngest player to score 200 points at the tender age of 19. When he was 21, he was the youngest player to captain a Stanley Cup-winning team.

Sidney Crosby

In 2008 Ovechkin set the record for most goals in a season by a right winger with 65 tallies. Eight years later he moved up to 33rd on the career goals list. At 525 goals, though, he was still 369 behind Gretzky's record of 894.

During the 2015–16 season, Los Angeles Kings goalie Jonathan Quick recorded his 41st and 42nd career shutouts. That may be a long way from Martin Brodeur's 125, but it set the record for a goalie born in the United States. It beat the previous mark of 40 held by John Vanbiesbrouck and Frank Brimsek. In 2012 Quick led the Kings to the Stanley Cup title with a .946 save percentage and a 1.41 goals-against average in the postseason. Those stand as the best playoff numbers for a goalie who played in more than 10 postseason games.

Brett Hull

CAREER GOALS

1. **Wayne Gretzky** (Oilers, Kings, Blues, Rangers)	894
2. **Gordie Howe** (Red Wings, Whalers)	801
3. **Jaromir Jagr** (Penguins, Capitals, Rangers, Flyers, Stars, Bruins, Devils, Panthers)	749
4. **Brett Hull** (Flames, Blues, Stars, Red Wings, Coyotes)	741
5. **Marcel Dionne** (Red Wings, Kings, Rangers)	731

Jagr stats through 2015–16 season

GLOSSARY

assist—a pass that leads to a goal; in hockey, up to two assists can be awarded on any goal

blueliner—a nickname for a defenseman

compile—to put together in a collection

determined—having a firm or fixed purpose

dramatic—greatly affecting people's attention or emotions

era—a period of time

fazed—afraid or uncertain

feat—an outstanding achievement

hat trick—three goals by one player in a single game

point—in hockey, a goal or an assist

revolutionizing—changing something in a big way

shootout—a contest of penalty shots used to decide a tie game

statistician—someone who collects and studies numbers and statistics

READ MORE

Frederick, Shane. *Six Degrees of Sidney Crosby.* Six Degrees of Sports. North Mankato, Minn.: Capstone Press, 2015.

Herman, Gail. *Who Is Wayne Gretzky?* Who Was ...? New York: Grosset & Dunlap, 2015.

Myers, Dan. *Hockey Trivia.* Sports Trivia Minneapolis: Abdo Pub., 2016.

INTERNET SITES

FactHound offers a safe, fun way to find Internet sites related to this book. All of the sites on FactHound have been researched by our staff.

Here's all you do:
Visit *www.facthound.com*

Type in this code: 9781515737582

Super-cool stuff!

Check out projects, games and lots more at
www.capstonekids.com

INDEX